GLOBAL REACH, LOCAL TOUCH

How to Win the Game of Importing and Distributing Italian Gourmet Food

GLOBAL REACH, LOCAL TOUCH

How to Win the Game of Importing
and Distributing Italian Gourmet Food

MARIANO MERCADANTE

Worldwide Publishing by
Pendown Press

PENDOWN PRESS

An ISO 9001 & ISO 14001 Certified Co.,

Regd. Office: 2525/193, 1st Floor, Onkar Nagar-A, Tri Nagar, Delhi-110035

Ph.: 09350849407, 09312235086

E-mail: info@pendownpress.com

Branch Office: 1A/2A, 20, Hari Sadan, Ansari Road, Daryaganj, New Delhi-110002

Ph.: 011-45794768

Website: PendownPress.com

First Edition: 2022

Price: ₹1999/-

ISBN: 978-93-5554-429-2

All Rights Reserved

All the ideas and thoughts in this book are given by the author and he is responsible for the treatise, facts and dialogues used in this book. He is also responsible for the used pictures and the permission to use them in this book. Copyright of this book is reserved with the author. The publisher does not have any responsibility for the above-mentioned matters. No part of this publication may be reproduced, distributed, or transmitted in any form or by any means, including photocopying, recording, or other electronic or mechanical methods, without the prior written permission of the publisher and author.

Layout and Cover Designed by Pendown Graphics Team

Printed and Bound in India by Thomson Press India Ltd.

Content

Thanking Amazing People

Sometimes we take for granted the wonderful people we are surrounded by who help and support us through our journey.

This book was possible thanks to all the people who contributed to it significantly, consciously or even unconsciously.

I would like to thank them all from the bottom of my heart.

My wife Irene, an inexhaustible source of gentleness, my life partner and my inspiration through my journey. With her great wisdom, she is always capable of bringing out the best in me.

My children Caterina and Giuliano, the joy of my life, they don't know yet, but they are an outstanding contribution to my motivation to get things done.

My sister Milena, who honoured me by joining our Food Business in recent years, is a master example of professionalism and dedication. Thank you for all the precious help.

My parents (blessing their Souls) taught me the grit and how important it is not to give up and overcome obstacles through our journey.

All the Saporalia staff, whose hard and relentless work is allowing us to grow year after year. Thanks to their dedication, we have the chance to participate in many important projects.

In particular, special thanks to Linda, who contributed in a big way to the finalization of this book

My past and present mentors, thank you for all the continuous great guidance and for leading people by example, through determination and humility: Mr. Guido Bonino, Mr. Istvan Kapitany, Mr. Anand Bajoria and Mr. Bernard Hofstein "Maestro."

My Business Partner and co-shareholder in the Energy and Mobility Lines of Business, Walter Potì, companion of many past, present and future Business challenges leading to great results, a great example of leading through competence and high determination.

All the people (direct employees as well as external resources, such as Agents and Partners) working in our operational Companies who belong to my little Group.

All my colleagues and coaches who I had the luck to meet during my journey in big Corporations before becoming an entrepreneur.

Last but not least Mr. Dinesh Verma and the Pendown Content & Editorial Team, for all the help, patience and guidance through the creation and publication of this book.

Every good piece of work always comes from strong teamwork, people who get on well together and produce great performance and results.

A Heart-to-Heart to Begin With!

"Italian Gourmet Food is currently experiencing its greatest and steepest growing curve in decades. In the last year, the export of Italian food products has seen a whopping increase of 9% for a total of 52 billion euros. This is becoming possible thanks to the increasing spending power of the middle-class population in many parts of the world. And also because people are becoming more and more careful about what they eat. They want to get not just healthy food, but also something which is tasty, elegant and something that matches their food and lifestyle habits."

— **Mariano Mercadante**

Founder of Saporalia Italian Gourmet Food

The Essence of My Journey and this Book

This book is for all of you who are dealing with food and beverage import and distribution.

I am an entrepreneur like you. We are all in the business of finding and retaining good customers in the best possible way by serving them and providing them with sure-fire solutions for their problems and struggles.

In the past decade, I have observed that Italian Gourmet Food has a great potential of being about to explode and set a new amazing trend all over the world. It is truly the case, as we have seen and are seeing.

Expo 2015 in Milan was just the detonator of this phenomenon. Just one year before this Universal Exhibition, I had funded my Company, Saporalia, aiming to help all those Importers and Distributors who were (or would have been) dealing with Italian Food, providing them with easy tools and concrete solutions in order to succeed in importing and distributing it.

Importers and Distributors are the essence of a local economy as they make it possible to get things that otherwise would not be available.

When we created Saporalia almost ten years ago, we thought our message and our value proposition would be understood easily.

We were wrong!

In fact, when we started the Saporalia journey, many people were sceptical. In order to make sure that a potential Saporalia Customer clearly sees the value we can add, it takes time.

However, in spite of the challenges, we kept working patiently, and today Saporalia has revolutionized the way to export Italian Gourmet Food, making it accessible and available in a better and more agile way.

Importers and Distributors around the world were used to buying Italian Food directly from producers, thinking it was the most efficient way. This can work when you buy from big industrial companies, but it is greatly inefficient if it is about Gourmet Artisanal Food, where you have to deal with multiple laboratories, which are great artisans producing amazing delicacies but don't have the time and resources to manage a structured and smooth export process. Yes, because if an Importer or Distributor wanted to buy, let's say, twenty different SKUs among Antipasti, Truffle and Sweet categories (for example), they would

- deal with at least four laboratories
- respect MOQ for each SKU
- place an order for each laboratory
- get certificates and manage bureaucracy for each laboratory
- manage logistics and delivery for each laboratory
- pay four invoices
- and so on

What Saporalia did was to democratize and facilitate Italian Gourmet Food, from Artisans to the world.

Our products are craft-produced/hand-made by food Artisans who are based in small hidden towns all over the various corners and locations of the Italian Peninsula, using traditional and manual methods of production, giving a big added value which is missing in any other classic industrial kind of product. Therefore, our products cannot be compared with other industrial-quality products.

- > 1000 SKUs available.
- No MOQ for the majority of the references.
- Consolidated different products at pallet level (mixed pallet or even half missed pallet).
- Custom and logistic bureaucracy, no stress.

- Great innovation (see, for example, our Balsamic Vinegar to bite, launched in 2022).

- Specific Marketing Support in Saporalia Customer's Market/s.

I have chosen to be courageous and clearly talk about this topic, to share our view and our way, and this is the first and unique book which is focusing on importing and distributing Italian Gourmet Food. We don't want to reach everybody with this book. We want to reach and help only you who are indeed at some point in the process of achieving success through importing and/or distributing Italian Gourmet Food.

I know you realize all of the facts illustrated above, and, honestly, I cannot wait to start working with you and help you make your customers so happy... I know it takes time to try a new supplier, but no worries, we are here whenever you are ready.

But one thing that is crystal clear in my mind and in the mind of each and every member of Saporalia is: that the customers that are choosing our products and services will always get the BEST that we can offer, the BEST effort at the top of our possibilities, without any conflict of interest and without any filter.

Guaranteed. No compromise!

So, in this book, I have tried to trace what it takes to successfully deal with Italian Gourmet Food, and I have written it all by keeping Importers and Distributors in mind. This book is especially for you.

Best regards,

– Mariano Mercadante

Chapter 1

What is Gourmet Food?

To be truly successful at something, it is essential to first understand the subject. Therefore, to begin with, let's understand what Gourmet Food is.

Let's start by saying that food is the only "consumer good" that we put inside our body and not outside, and therefore it is much more important than all the other goods. Behind Gourmet Food, there is a world of culture, traditions, and values.

Though the word Gourmet is an objective term in the world of food, its meaning, I feel, is subjective. What is "Gourmet" for a person who prepares it may not be so for one who eats it. However, having said that, let me specify that there are certain ingredients associated with the word Gourmet.

Based on these ingredients, Gourmet Food is prepared with the intention of enhancing taste, feeling, and sensory pleasure to a new (elevated) level of eating experience.

So, you can say that Gourmet Food is an experience!

Gourmet Food is not like any other food; it is an experience in itself. It is a journey to the root of the place where that food was produced. It is an elegant and tasty creation that stimulates the visual senses as well as the taste buds. It is something that people look forward to having as a reward after a day of a big effort. It is also something that you would want to showcase to impress the guests that you have invited for dinner on a Saturday evening.

Gourmet food is also about history: when we tell our customers about our products, I also add some anecdotes about their history that sometimes even date back to ancient Roman times. This is because we are not only selling Italian Gourmet products but rather pieces of Italian history.

Italians are so proud of their typical dishes and products because they are a fundamental part of our culture and lifestyle; it's not only about nourishment. While eating, we know that we are enjoying something that has been passed from generation to generation, keeping the original taste and quality intact.

Whenever our customers purchase our products, they purchase fragments of Italian history, and who knows, maybe even Julius Caesar consumed the same products. Isn't that incredible?

Keeping it fresh is the secret!

There is a critical secret to getting Gourmet Food just right. That secret is fresh food.

If you are in the business of Gourmet Food or if your customers like good Italian fresh food, then that's great to know.

However, to do well and keep your customers happy, you will have to select a supplier who is pretty strong in trading fresh products and delivering them wherever in the world it is required to be delivered on time.

Achieving this timely delivery of fresh food globally is a challenging task. There is a complex logistic environment to be managed around fresh food, such as the right delivery partners, precise delivery, customs-related bureaucracy, maintenance of a guaranteed temperature chain, etc.

Some examples of the fresh food products that we are talking about would be buffalo mozzarella (PDO), stracciatella, burrata, all kinds of Italian cheese, or other fresh products like cured meats, fresh truffles and mushrooms etc.

When this is the kind of list of ingredients that you need to procure for your Gourmet Food enterprise, then it is definitely too difficult to deal with each and every small artisanal laboratory as they are too many and too fragmented throughout the whole Peninsula.

The key is to choose and deal with a single partner who is capable of offering a wide variety of products and can help to simplify your business with a solid interface through the beautiful world of Italian Gourmet Food.

Fresh products can increase your profit significantly

Many of my colleagues thought I was crazy when I focused on specializing in managing fresh food. I knew it was one of the most challenging tasks in today's food industry, I mean, controlling the product quality throughout the whole Food supply chain, etc..

We went for this bet: we integrated food quality into the decision-making process through production and distribution as well as our food supply chain, starting from our laboratories, of course.

We created a new methodology to model and manage fresh food production and logistics and properly integrate that in multi laboratories, programs and distribution planning, a real key approach for ushaving tens of laboratories to coordinate!

Quite an important part of our products is fresh or perishable food: dairy products, cheese, cured meat, meat, fish, vegetables, and truffles.

So what did I mean by **"How to increase profit with fresh products?"**

I meant that if you are buying fresh truffle from somebody who is not capable of making sure that you receive it properly fresh, you are losing the margin for sure as you cannot ask your customers what you should, in terms of pricing for that Gourmet delicacy.

The same goes for delicate dairy like burrata, stracciatella, etc.

Gourmet Food vs Industrial Food

At this point, it is clear that gourmet food offers a unique sensory experience that is impossible to imitate.

This characteristic is due to the time, attention and dedication of the craftsmen during the production process of the delicacy.

This mastery disappears when we treat industrial foods since the purpose of the two products is different.

Saporalia is betting on the possibility of giving space to small Italian artisans and creating market opportunities for them in foreign countries that are almost inaccessible to them. Therefore, we only propose and promote products of excellence that are handcrafted and which help in feeling good, far from industrial chains.

The purpose of gourmet products is to offer a unique experience, while the purpose of industrial products is to produce products that are accessible to most consumers.

Since the purpose of the two products is different, the quality of the raw materials used, as well as the times and methods of production, also differ.

The ingredients of the gourmet products are, in fact, of the highest quality. This doesn't mean that industrial products can't be tasty, but they will always lack a certain nuance of flavour.

Here is a short example: our brand often introduces new products, and a little while ago we put on the market a new type of breads ticks.

Breads ticks, in general, are not a difficult product to find, even in the supermarket, so my customers rightly ask me: how are ours different?

Here, at the risk of sounding arrogant, I reply that our breads ticks taste like real fragrant bread and not just plain water and flour.

This little anecdote is not aimed at convincing you that we have the best products. **It is merely meant to emphasize that there is a real difference between industrial and Gourmet products.**

However, the limitation of Gourmet products is that, unfortunately, they are not for everyone, given the lower availability of excellent raw materials. But it has to be this way. Otherwise, we wouldn't be talking about Gourmet Food.

In addition to availability, the exclusivity of Gourmet Food is also due to its higher prices compared to industrial products.

For this reason, the mission we have set ourselves is to offer Gourmet Food at more accessible prices, but still less economical than industrial ones, in order to democratize it and make Italian Gourmet Food more accessible.

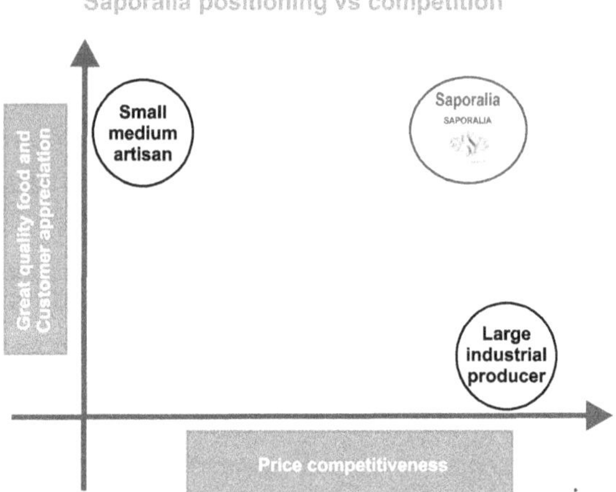

Chapter 2

What does it take to Import real Italian Gourmet Food?

As I promised, with the secrets I share in this book, I will make it easy and effortless for you to be greatly successful and profitable as an Importer/Distributor of Gourmet Italian Food.

To fulfil this promise beginning with this chapter, I will share in detail all the criteria, tips and techniques to be successful in this industry.

Choosing an innovative – partner to add value to your operations.

Let's start with an example:

The worst tavern and a starred establishment share the same name: "Restaurant".

Similarly, even fake and real export experts of Italian food products share the same name: "Exporters".

How do you, in both cases, distinguish one from the other?

In the case of restaurants, a criterion exists.

1. The stars

2. Online reviews

In the first case, an external body certifies whether or not the restaurant deserves to be awarded the star and how many stars. In the second, it is the customers themselves who establish the appreciation through online reviews.

After that, when customers reserve a table in a starred restaurant, they know that they won't spend less than €150/200, and they know that they will receive a whole series of special treatments.

If they book a table in a non-starred restaurant but full of positive reviews, they know it is likely to be fine. And if their preferences go to the worst tavern instead, they know the quality to expect and the costs.

On the basis of what, instead, does a customer choose an Italian Gourmet Food supplier?

To successfully import real Italian Gourmet Food, it is important to choose an innovation-addicted partner who can export Italian Food products directly from small and medium producers exclusively to you, the importers and distributors.

They must be able to do it in a way that will allow you to stay ahead of your competitors. They should always be able to supply you with products that are setting the market trends. Products that others will try to copy and follow.

But you will always be the first in your market to offer these when dealing with an innovative partner.

Your partner should be able to create and share the newest products of the Italian artisanal tradition-The food of tomorrow, while also owning a wide range of conventional Gourmet Food products.

In the following chapters, I will share with you all the necessary criteria that will help you choose the right export partner and be a super successful Italian Gourmet Food importer/distributor.

Bonus: Example of how to launch an innovative product, watch this webinar on Youtube to see the Balsamic Vinegar to bite example.

Just scan this QR code and get your bonus.

Chapter 3

Choosing a Partner that has a Variety of Products and is easy to Work with

As an importer/distributor, there will be many options of partners available to you, but the difference between the rest and the best is very simple and very essential at the same time:

First of all you should choose an export partner with whom you can order just what you need (there should be no boundaries of minimum order quantity).

Also, your partner should be able to offer you access to a wide variety of Italian Gourmet Food in every possible size to choose from. This will enable you to pick just the ones that you think are most appropriate for your business and for your customers by selecting the quantity you need.

The partner you choose should have at least close to 1000 products on offer.

If you want an example of what variety means, here is a list of just a few Antipasti items (SKUs) offered by Saporalia.

- Anchovy stuffed peppers

- Tuna stuffed peppers

- Tuna stuffed yellow peppers
- Semi-dry tomatoes
- Grilled onions in oil
- Grilled artichokes in oil
- Grilled aubergines in oil
- Grilled peppers in oil
- Grilled courgettes in oil
- Seasoned tomatoes
- Capers berries
- Capers in salt
- Capers in brine
- Seasoned lampascioni
- Giant lupins
- Marinated Tropea onions
- Sun-dried tomatoes pesto alla Genovese
- Mixed mushrooms
- Anchovies al Verde
- Spanish anchovies
- Green olives
- Spicy crushed green olives
- Super mammouth olives
- Olives pitted flavored black olives
- Seasoned baresane olives

- Barese black olives
- Pitted olives with capers
- Pitted tomato-stuffed olives
- Sweet green bella cerignola
- Bella di cerigniola black
- Oven passoluni Calabria
- Olives gaeta
- Olives pitted black Calabrian olives
- Peasant olives
- Boscaiola olives
- Almond olives
- Black Taggiasca olives in brine
- Live riviera seasoned

These are just a few examples..

Further, we suggest choosing a partner who is well organized and categorized their products into various heads, such as:

- ➢ Truffle products
- ➢ Antipasti
- ➢ Cheese
- ➢ Dairy
- ➢ Cured meat
- ➢ Pates
- ➢ Vegetables

> ➢ Chocolate

> ➢ EVO oil from different Regions

> ➢ Vinegars

> ➢ Pasta and Fresh Pasta

> ➢ Desserts

> ➢ etc

This will save you a lot of time and effort while choosing and ordering.

Chapter 4

Choosing a Partner who Supports you Completely with Marketing & Promotional Tools

Too often, it happens that after you buy the products that you had previously selected, you receive them in your warehouse, and then you are just left alone with the duty to sell them to your Customers.

To ensure success, market penetration and customer retention, it is essential to choose a partner **that differentiates themselves strongly** in comparison with other food suppliers in terms of marketing support in addition to supplying quality products.

They should be able to educate, empower and support you with content that will help you to increase the awareness, knowledge and popularity of these Gourmet products among your customers.

A great partner who is truly interested in a win-win co-operation will **create & provide you with**

- content that can be published on social channels;
- videos that can be used in many contexts;

- marketing sheets related to specific products with details about how to use/prepare/taste certain products and recipes;

- dummy examples of our products that you can display in your stores;

- host a joint webinar through which you can educate your audience about a specific product (launch) and/or category.

While you may have your own marketing department and perhaps be already very active on this (and that is great!) but why not save time and cost with great material already prepared by the exporter, specifically on their products to **help you to increase your sales?**

At Saporalia, for example, we created some material for one of our Importers (actually requested by its direct distributor). It was all about pictures of mixed products that we created for different purposes, such as

- display in stores for training during customers' tasting;

- content for social media (you can see the final exact shape of some of them), especially Instagram and Facebook;

- content for the website;

- specific size content for a blog;

And here is the feedback from this customer:)

Dear Mariano,

Thanks always for your support.

I shall surely share display images and sampling images.

Also, it would be of great support if you share some dummy products with which we want to create an in-store experience.

We would require dummies of the following:

Cheese wheel or any Cheese related products.

Dummy meat (cold cuts) which we can hang in our meat section to create impact.

Any other dummy products which are available and that you can supply

Thank you

HK

Marketing material and good content in any of its form is essential for you as a distributor because it helps you to increase your authority and differentiate yourself from your competitors in your market (or markets).

100% ORGANIC DIRECTLY FROM ITALY
SAPORALIA ORGANIC CHEESE
100% ORGANIC

100% ORGANIC DIRECTLY FROM ITALY
SAPORALIA
Available in our stores
SAPORALIA ORGANIC CHEESE
ENVIRONMENT FRIENDLY
100% ORGANIC
NO HARM TO NATURE
Organic
100% ORGANIC

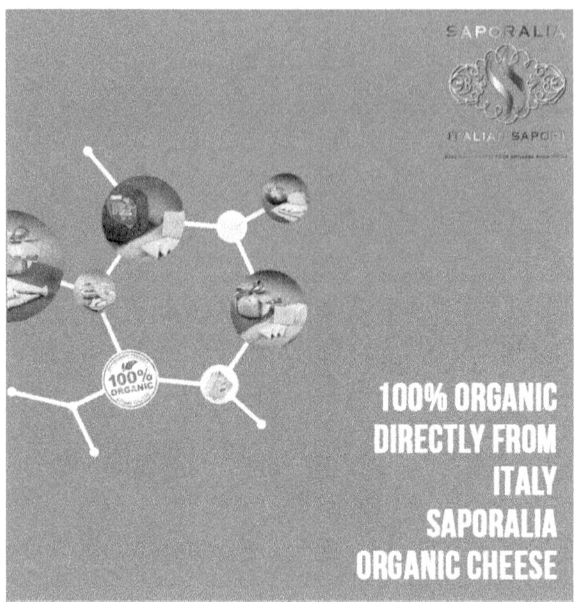
SAPORALIA
ITALIAN SAPORI
100% ORGANIC
DIRECTLY FROM
ITALY
SAPORALIA
ORGANIC CHEESE
100% ORGANIC

Chapter 5

Evolution of a Great Idea –
The Logistic Approach: Choose
a Logistically Sound Partner

Without logistics excellence, you can't go too far!

It is key to have procedures in place and be perfectly organized in order to be able to reach every place all over the world in the quickest way, maintaining perfect product quality while dealing with bureaucracy.

So, choose a partner who is logistically sound and capable of taking care of the entire goods delivery process, starting from the attention it takes to create packaging, up to the delivery of the goods, constantly monitoring the proper operations of all shipments, as a guarantee of safety and quality of service, in order to best meet the customer's needs.

Your export partner should be able to manage the end-to-end process from their warehouse to your door wherever in the world you may be through current competitive market conditions.

Yet they should be flexible enough to allow you to choose logistic plans that work for you, like alternatively choosing to ask for the products at to be shipped only till any Italian port (or even at their warehouse), and you manage all the rest on your own. Or, for that matter, an arrangement in between these two arrangements.

They should be able to arrange Sea Freight, exporting through navigating from all Italian ports to all destinations in the world, providing maximum customs and operative assistance, also assistance at destination port through their agencies, on forwarding to domicile/to door.

They should be able to arrange Airfreight, both through controlled temperature*and ambient temperature.

(*this is not with the normal cool cover, which exposes the pallets to the risk of warming up during transits or waiting slots, they should be able to manage that with solutions that guarantee the temperature whatever happens, till it gets into the customer's hands.)

They should also be able to arrange Carriage by Truck and Surface Transportation where possible and needed.

As we all know, packing fragile goods, such as agri-food products, requires great attention to the design of the packaging and in the handling of the goods, especially when pallets are mixed (this is something that requires operational excellence, and only a select few can offer this) and need to be created with different products of different sizes, which are more easily exposed to the risk of damage.

For example, we at Saporalia studied, researched and then developed the most suitable packaging, which consists of the use of a sturdy cardboard box which contains the individually packaged products inside. In order to ensure further security, the whole is then packed with ultra-reinforced protection.

That is why you must be careful who you import your Gourmet Italian Food from. It is of crucial importance that the partner selling a Gourmet product must also ensure that its transport is flawless. For them, quality should be the guiding force in every phase.

By choosing the right partner, you will be sure that all the products you ordered will arrive safe and sound to their destinations, and you need not spend sleepless nights filled with worry over the fate of the consignment!

Chapter 6

Choose a Partner who is Willing to Consider Exclusivity

The Gourmet Food industry is exclusive in nature and is considered to be in a class of its own. Having exclusivity on some products and areas at least would be great for your branding and sales, and perceived value.

So associating with a partner with a wide range of products is essential for you to ask and for them even to be able to consider giving you exclusivity.

Apart from having the range to offer exclusivity, your export partner should be willing to consider offering exclusivity. They should be open to analyzing the market, segments and channels where you operate and the products that you would like to select.

Selling some Gourmet Food products with exclusive rights in your market can give you a great advantage over your competition as you will be able to claim that you are the only operator able to sell/distribute those products.

Chapter 7

Choose a Partner who is Eager to know you (and your business) exceptionally well and to Focus on you!

For a great working relationship leading to smooth operations, which will translate into sales and profits, it is essential that your partner should make an effort to know you well and should focus on supporting your growth on the basis of your feedback.

Wouldn't you love to receive an email like this!!!

- My name is Maria Eugenia D'Orazio, and I am the Sales Representative for Saporalia.

- As a subscriber to our email distribution list, I would love to hear your opinion and feedback on our work, product and content!

- Do you find our newsletters and material interesting? Do we cover topics (products, services) that are interesting to you?

- We care a lot about this, and it is very important to always improve in order to offer the best service possible.

- Is there anything you would like to learn more directly from me or with a colleague of the team?

- Make your appointment directly with us (it is free and without any obligation, of course).

- Just choose the time that suits you best, so we can understand how to be even more useful to you.

- You can make an appointment by clicking the button below.

- Thank you, and I'm looking forward to having a chat with you.

This shows your partner's genuine desire to be able to serve you better.

Or imagine receiving an email like this:

➢ We know who you are!

➢ From this side of the screen, I can't really know who exactly will be reading this email apart from the certainty that my words will be read by people passionate about food and entrepreneurs who are (or are preparing to be) very active in the Gourmet Food Business. There is another thing that I am so sure about.

➢ That whoever is reading these lines is a person keen to offer the greatest products and the greatest service to their customers.

➢ So if you recognize yourself in this brief description, we want to help you to succeed in this purpose.

➢ OK, but how?

[Then, a partner who is sure of their worth because they have worked hard and humbly to offer you the best product/service would go on to explain what they bring to the table.]

We can serve you through our agility and flexibility with:

- \> 1000 products (SKUs) available.

- No MOQ for the majority of the references.

- Possibility to consolidate a multitude of products at pallet level (mixed pallet or even half mixed pallet).

- Zero stress through custom and logistic bureaucracy and process.

- Continuous innovation (see, for example, our new Solid Balsamic Vinegar recently launched).

- Specific Marketing support in the market/s where you operate.

This is what we do. This is why we are sure we know who you are.

Therefore a partner who works hard to understand you will be your biggest support system on the path to success.

Chapter 8

Choose a Partner who knows the Italian Peninsula & its Food Excellences like the Back of their Hand

The Italian Peninsula, with its diverse culture and cuisine, is a treasure house of Gourmet Food products right from Aosta to Trapani, from Bari to Ventimiglia and from Trieste to Reggio Calabria!

Your partner should have the ability and capacity to select and curate some of the greatest food excellences of our wonderful Peninsula.

They should be able to make available to you a rich catalogue to select products best placed to have success in your market and geography.

Just think about how many types of cheese alone are available in Italy.

I think it can easily be said that you can find a different kind of cheese in any province (not region, but province) you go to!

There are many ways to use the same ingredients, and there also exist quite many climate differences between Italian regions; but there is more to say about that.

If you look for Italy on a world map, it is easy to spot it due to its original shape, located in the South of Europe.

Its territory is long and tight, is sort of amazing and is attached to the rest of Europe through its highest mountains in the north: the Alps.

In the centre, it is sort of kept together by the Apennines and the South, and the islands are surrounded by the Mediterranean sea.

Three very different kinds of climates, lands and cultures in the same Country.

This explains such a deep diversity in the food production and approach.

A smart and knowledgeable supplier who is well versed with the land, culture and cuisine can take advantage of all this magnificence and put together a wide list of these products.

You want a typical cheese which is produced in a remote province in the South of Italy? Your supplier should be able to say: Sure! We have it!

Chapter 9

Delivery Time FAQs to Test your Partner's Responsiveness

Here are some questions, the answers to which will tell you how responsive your partner is and whether you should continue with the relationship or find a more responsive supplier.

How many days do you need to wait from the day you place an order until the moment your products arrive at your warehouse?

This is a tricky question, I know. And actually, of course, it all depends on the distance and the type of transport of the goods!

In fact, I deliberately posed the question in the wrong way.

The right wording for the questions would be –

- What's your supplier lead time?

- How many days go from the day you place an order till the moment your products Leave Your Supplier's warehouse?

These are the key questions!

From these parameters, you can evaluate your supplier response rate.

There would be many different values in various countries.

The answer to the question may vary from 3-5 days for more structured companies up until even 10-15 days for smaller enterprises, plus of course, the time that it will take for the goods to be transported and delivered to you.

I think this is an important aspect because the faster your supplier is in refurbishing your warehouse, the better the situation you will have in terms of avoiding problems with your stock and also for you to have sustainable management of products' quantities in your warehouse in order to not increase your stock too much.

Interesting Fact: you may (or may not) know that in Italy, the stock is taxed by authorities and by the government (*I am not aware if this is the case in any other country, please do let me know if you have the same problem as I am curious*) so all the producers and exporters tend to have stock at a real minimum level and manage the production and the acquisition of the products only once they receive the new order from customers

This, of course, doesn't help your stock management and makes the product's delivery timing a bit too long --> Not good!

A good and trustworthy supplier will work their way around it by trying to identify the recurrence of ordered products' quantities (not only the ordering frequency, which is not always in our or your control but defining a sort of standard ordered quantity) and when this is defined, they will make sure their warehouse will always maintain that quantity of products you may/will order plus 30% of them in case you need more.

Obviously, they will be taking some risks here because a customer may not order those products, but I can tell you this makes a difference with a lot of customers in terms of timing in sending the goods when receiving the new order.

Your partner should be able to understand your standardized orders and have the goods leave their warehouse the same day when receiving the order in the morning till 12 (CET – Central Europe Time zone), or the day after if the order arrives when it is already afternoon for them.

It has to be emphasized that another important value to take into consideration is the shelf life. Of course, for short shelf life products keeping stock is not possible without a strict plan, so ensure that the majority of products in your supplier's range have a shelf life of close to 36 months.

So, what about you? Are you happy with your supplier's lead times?

Chapter 10

Choose a Partner with Integrity

I want to share with you a problem that can happen with Italian food producers. Especially if you are dealing with small producers. I want to be clear, if you are not selling Italian products and you are not planning to do it, this is not interesting for you. If you are selling Italian products and you are dealing with industrial corporations, this is not interesting for you as well.

This is relevant when you only deal with small Italian producers. If you deal with them and they only speak Italian, this is relevant for you: So here's the issue: these people are in love with what they do and what they produce; they live for it. Every day. They may not be so good in marketing relatively; they may also be having challenges in communication because they are basically artisans of excellence and not marketers. They are not poets who can eloquently praise their products. And this is how it is supposed to be.

Not all the doughnuts ("ciambelle", as we call them) come out with a hole; it's an Italian saying that describes the situation. It means that even if you normally produce excellence, sometimes things may go wrong. It happens! Sometimes things can go wrong. But when something happens, instead of being reluctant to admit that something went wrong, your partner must have the integrity to take responsibility and sort out the situation with integrity.

Let me explain this better with an example of how we handled a situation like this when it happened to us. There is a small producer of Panettone – a Christmas cake we have in Italy – who makes an amazing product, he has even won prizes from magazines and so on. This is normally the type of producer we are dealing with. We sent 150 Panettones to one of our German distributors around the 10th of December 2017, and it was a big order. It is not an industrial product, it's a premium product, so it's not cheap. They perfectly arrived at the destination, everything was OK as usual, our distributor started to sell in the following days, but it turned out that some Panettones had a problem: the Panettone with Pistachios was cooked a bit less than it was supposed to or it was exposed to too much humidity…i don't know. Nobody will ever know; it happens.

So, our distributor's customers discovered that, and they told the distributor. They returned the product, so one day the consumer of the gourmet shop in Munich returned this Panettone, claiming that it was not well cooked. We don't sell industrial products; as we always say, we are selling artisanal excellence. So they are not always perfect. What's the point of this story? Well, these things happen. Not often, luckily, but sometimes it happens.

And what did we do? We were in emergency mode. We are used to hoping for the best but expecting the worst. So, we immediately sent our truck to take all those Panettones back, and let's be clear, even if there was the possibility that the problem was about 1 or 2 Panettone, we took back all of them. Just to be sure. We reimbursed the distributor, and we asked for the contact details of the Gourmet shop in Munich, and we sent them some Panettone: with chocolate, with pistachio, a classic one, with extra-virgin olive oil and one with exotic fruits. We sent two boxes. One was for the shop, and one for the consumer. All this recovery plan took place in 3 days. Logistics helped since it was in Europe, while in Asia, for example, it would have taken longer.

The shop was impressed with how the distributor, and us, dealt with this issue so quickly, and they were very thankful. The consumer was also very impressed, and he was happy that the Panettone was as good as it was supposed to be, and he had the opportunity to also try the other kinds. So everyone was happy, and our distributor had the chance to increase his business thanks to this issue.

You always have to imagine that there can be a crisis if you want to be able to deal with it. The point, in the end, is that issues happen, and it can be tricky. For us, customers come first, always, and we try to deal with that. If you are dealing with Italian suppliers, you may have issues, but it is important how you deal with them. Solve it, make your customer happy, and that's it.

Chapter 11

OK, Let's Bust Some Myths

Myth #1 – Italian Gourmet Food is Expensive

Yes, Italian Gourmet Food is expensive but worth it. It's all about finding the right supplier.

Working with specialized Gourmet Italian Food in the past years, I have developed some good marketing and brand positioning skills, which are essential to thrive in this industry and I have realized that with the right positioning and branding, dealing in Italian Gourmet Food can actually be very profitable for the importers and distributors.

How does it work? This is a real game changer: a Gourmet Italian Food supplier capable of helping you to position these products in your markets, someone who can offer a detailed consultancy in terms of marketing and brand positioning and support in implementing a Direct Response Marketing campaign for your potential customers and help you in finding your unicity for your preferred customer targets.

This will go a long way and will ensure that your Italian Gourmet products will have a high acceptance in your market and help you to sell even more of them to your customers.

This works, and this process is really fulfilling for both partners: we sell great food which is good for the human body and spirit; while selling more.

Here are some examples of what we mean about your supplier creating some marketing material for customers.

Yes, good food is great, and we understand our partner must support us in marketing to sell more and be profitable.

OK, but we still need to talk about the price!

OK, yes, your partner needs to be very competitive in pricing while offering the best of Italian food production and quality!

To be able to be competitive, they would need a pretty big buying power with small Italian artisanal laboratories (in or even own shares of the laboratory and have direct involvement in the production).

The scale of operations of your partner has a significant impact on your success.

For sure!

Your success as an entrepreneur in the food and beverage industry is measured by several indicators, some are subjective, like the quality of the food that you sell or the look of the packages and of the products themselves, but some others are very objective, such as profit generation that is your oxygen to sustain your business and thrive.

That is why it is important for your partner to be able to help these products be positioned as very high-quality products with extremely convenient price ratios that allow you to offer the best products at the right price.

Choosing the right supplier is indeed a delicate task because you need someone big enough to buy/produce tons of products; and own shares of the laboratory so that they can give premium quality at competitive prices, has a high rated feedback about the service yet smart and small enough to be agile without any unnecessary fixed costs, hence always ultra-competitive.

This allows us to offer you the best Italian products at a highly competitive price.

Myth #2 – You need to buy everything directly from producers

This has been a common belief for a lot of time, till Saporalia came around.

As I wrote at the beginning of this book, Importers and Distributors around the world used to buy Italian food directly from producers, thinking it was the most efficient way.

This can work when you buy from big industrial companies, but it is greatly inefficient if it is about gourmet artisanal food, where you have to deal with multiple laboratories, which are great artisans producing amazing delicacies but don't have the time and resources to manage a structured and smooth export process. Yes, because if an importer or distributor wanted to buy, let's say 20 different SKUs among Antipasti, Truffle and Sweet categories (for example), they would

- deal with at least 4 laboratories

- respect MOQ for each SKU

- place an order for each laboratory

- get certificates and manage bureaucracy for each laboratory

- manage logistics and delivery for each laboratory

- pay 4 invoices

- and so on…

What Saporalia did was to democratize Italian Gourmet Food, from Artisans to the world.

- > 1000 SKU available

Products are craft-produced/hand-made by food artisans who are based in small hidden towns all over the various corners and locations of the Italian Peninsula, using traditional and manual methods of production, giving a big added value which is missing in any other classic industrial kind of product. Therefore, our products cannot be compared with other industrial-quality products.

- No MOQ for the majority of the references

- Consolidated different products at pallet level (mixed pallet or even half missed pallet)

- Custom and logistic bureaucracy, no stress

- Great innovation (see for example our Balsamic Vinegar to bite, launched in 2022)

- Specific Marketing support in Saporalia Customer's Market/s

Those things are not immediately metabolized all together, it is about changing the status quo, it is about moving to the next level consistently.

Myth #3 – Italian Gourmet Food is Hard to Import

Italian Gourmet Food importing and distribution (including successful sales of it) can be effortless with the right supplier and keeping these important tips that I have discovered through my years of experience.

Tips to Remember:

✓ Each and every artisan doesn't speak very good English.

✓ 1 order, 1 delivery, 1 invoice, 1 payment for each of the producers.

- ✓ MOQ obligations for each of them.

- ✓ If you are Italian and live abroad, probably if you put 2 people on this job, you can manage to get it done.

- ✓ If you need Industrial products, I mean food from big corporations; obviously, it is another sport, so not applicable.

- ✓ But if you are a non-Italian in whatever market and like to have a wide variety of Italian Gourmet Food, then you need to deal with a careful supplier who can remove all the headaches around you with relation to these processes and put you in a position to succeed while importing and distributing it.

To Conclude it All

Importing and distributing Italian Gourmet Food is a wonderful job if you have the right partner.

Good intentions are not enough to combine 1. artisanal production (Gourmet) with 2. modern distribution; that is not a game for all; it is necessary to transform both of these aspects to make them 'compatible' with one another.

No agreement is possible between them except through a radical renewal of both. Saporalia's strategy lies in this renovation work.

To support the project, it has been necessary to develop a system that supports a competitive commercial and logistics chain in the market, integrating multiple levels of production and laboratories for the distribution of artisanal products at every point of the Globe.

Another important point is the prices. If Saporalia sticks to the prices and styles of the great boutiques of excellent food, it will have missed its essential mission of innovation and will be destined for modest and limited success to a niche clientele.

The purpose of this direction is to ensure the distribution aspect of the products (which remains the core business of the project because success depends on this optimization) has a sufficiently solid base.

Having to deal with small artisan producers, we cannot expect the level of organization and service offered by industrial companies. Saporalia laboratories are simply not used to put structure in the export activities.

In some cases, they do not even compile a detailed catalogue of their products, they do not maintain computerized warehouse management, they do not have long-term production plans, and they do not have a well-defined business strategy.

Managing relationships with traditional small producers implies building a personal relationship with each of them.

As Importer and/or Distributor, you should make sure to choose a partner who owns these above-mentioned competencies.

Finally, the Customers who choose to import and distribute Italian Gourmet Food are, on average, more competent and informed than the customers who deal with industrial products. They are capable of transferring this knowledge to their related customers either in Service or Retail and making them happy.

To preserve its image as a 'temple' of Italian gastronomy of excellence, Saporalia cannot afford any mistakes in the selection of products.

Saporalia is helping its Customers in a big way through specific and focussed Marketing Activities and by launching totally innovative (100% unique) products on a monthly basis that Customers will be able to have, on a sole basis, available in their market/s.

No one has ever written a book on how to be successful Importing and/or Distributing Italian Gourmet food anywhere in the world. We wanted to be of service to stand out and clearly talk about how we see this topic. I really hope we clarified and added value to this.

Our dozens and dozens of customers send us messages of the highest satisfaction, which is a privilege for us; it is a source of inexhaustible motivation.

So finally, thank you very much for reading this book. We hope you find it a source of inspiration.

Thanks to all our customers of yesterday, today and tomorrow.

We shall always endeavor to give you the best of the best of this service.

Wherever you are on the path to becoming a successful importer and distributor of Italian Gourmet Food, whether you are thinking of this business or you have just opened this business, or perhaps you have this business already established, whenever you feel ready to take the Italian Gourmet Food distribution business in your market to the next level, we are right here, ready to support you.

Reach out to us at:

Mariano Mercadante

info@saporalia.com

www.ingramcontent.com/pod-product-compliance
Lightning Source LLC
LaVergne TN
LVHW041240200726

843507LV00013B/2755